ALPHA BOOKS

JERUSALEM

NICOLA BARBER

Published by Evans Brothers Limited
2A Portman Mansions
Chiltern Street
London **W1U 6NR**

First published in paperback in 2003

© copyright in the text and illustrations Evans Brothers Limited 1999

First published 1999

Typeset by TJ Graphics
Printed in Hong Kong by Wing King Tong

British Library Cataloguing in Publication Data

Barber, Nicola
Jerusalem. - (Alpha books)
1. Jerusalem in Christianity - Juvenile literature
2. Jerusalem in Judaism - Juvenile literature
3. Jerusalem History - Juvenile literature
I. Title
956.9'422

ISBN 0 237 52567 4

Acknowledgements

Editor: Victoria Brooker
Design: Monica Chia and TJ Graphics
Production: Jenny Mulvanny
Consultants: Anne Clark, Maggie Everett and Khadijah Knight
Maps: Jillian Luff of Bitmap Graphics

This book is based on *Holy Cities Jerusalem* by Saviour Pirotta, first published by Evans Brothers in 1993.

VISIT OUR WEBSITE
Evans
www.evansbooks.co.uk

For permission to reproduce copyright material the author and publishers gratefully acknowledge the following:

Cover: (top left) Robert Harding Picture Library; (top right and back cover) Tony Souter, Hutchison Library; (bottom) Genut Audio Visual Productions, Israel;
Endpapers: Front - Christ's birthplace, Bethlehem - Douglas Pike, Bruce Coleman Limited; Back - the interior of the Dome of the Rock, Jerusalem - Tony Souter, Hutchison Library
Title page: A view of old Jerusalem taken through a chapel window on the Mount of Olives - Genut Audio Visual Productions, Israel
Contents page: One of the artist Marc Chagall's stained glass-windows found in the synagogue in Hadassah Hospital - Genut Audio Visual Productions, Israel

Page 6 (main picture) Robert Harding Picture Library (inset) Genut Audio Visual Productions, Israel; **page 8** (top) Robert Harding Picture Library (bottom) Simon McBride, Hutchison Library; **page 9** Robert Harding Picture Library **page 10** Tony Souter, Hutchison Library; **page 11** Ronald Sheridan, Ancient Art and Architecture Collection; **page 12,13, 14** Genut Audio Visual Productions, Israel; **page 15** Robert Harding Picture Library; **page 16** et archive; **page 17** Ronald Sheridan, Ancient Art and Architecture Collection; **page 18, 19, 20** Genut Audio Visual Productions, Israel; **page 21** (top) Hutchison Library (bottom) Genut Audio Visual Productions, Israel; **page 22, 23** Ronald Sheridan, Ancient Art and Architecture Collection; **page 24** Robert Harding Picture Library; **page 25** Genut Audio Visual Productions, Israel; **page 26** Melanie Friend, Hutchison Library; **page 27** Genut Audio Visual Productions, Israel; **page 28** (left) Robert Harding Picture Library (top) Genut Audio Visual Productions, Israel; **page 29** (left) Robert Harding Picture Library (right) Hutchison Library; **page 30** Genut Audio Visual Productions, Israel; **page 31** (left) Tony Souter, Hutchison Library (right) F. Jack Jackson, Robert Harding Picture Library; **page 32** (left) Tony Souter, Hutchison Library (top) Robert Harding Picture Library; **page 33** Robert Harding Picture Library; **page 34** (top) Genut Audio Visual Productions, Israel; (bottom) Ronald Sheridan, Ancient Art and Architecture Collection; **page 35** (bottom left and top right) Genut Audio Visual Productions, Israel; (inset) Robert Harding Picture Library; **page 36** Genut Audio Visual Productions, Israel; **page 37** (left) T. E. Clark, Hutchison Library (right) Ronald Sheridan, Ancient Art and Architecture Collection; **page 38** Genut Audio Visual Productions, Israel; **page 39** Robert Harding Picture Library; **page 40** Ronald Sheridan, Ancient Art and Architecture Collection; **page 41** Robert Harding Picture Library; **page 42** (top) Genut Audio Visual Productions, Israel; (bottom) Tony Souter, Hutchison Library; **page 43** Genut Audio Visual Productions, Israel;

Contents

Jerusalem the golden 6

The birth of Jerusalem 11

Sharing Jerusalem 14

Jerusalem lost 18

The Diaspora 22

A nation for the Jews 23

Jewish places of worship 24

Christian shrines and churches 28

Mosques of Jerusalem 32

Celebrations 34

Legends and traditions 36

Art and architecture 38

Food in Jerusalem 42

Important events 44

Index 46

Muslims usually say the words 'peace be upon him' after they say the Holy Prophet Muhammad's name. These words have been left out of this book for simplicity.

All words in **bold** are explained in the Key word boxes at the end of each chapter.

In this book, the letters CE are used after a date instead of AD appearing before it. CE means 'in the Common Era' or after the birth of Jesus Christ. So 1200 CE is the same as AD 1200. In the same way BCE, meaning 'Before the Common Era' is used instead of BC.

Jerusalem the golden

Jerusalem is a holy city for people of three religions, Christians, Jews and Muslims. Today the city is part of the Jewish State of Israel. But people of many different religions live in Jerusalem.

Jerusalem lies between the Mediterranean Sea and the Dead Sea (see map on page 7). To the west is the green countryside of Israel. To the east is the hot, dry Judean Desert.

► The Judean Desert is hot, dry and dusty.
▼ The buildings of Jerusalem are made from stone which glows golden in the early morning and late evening sunlight.

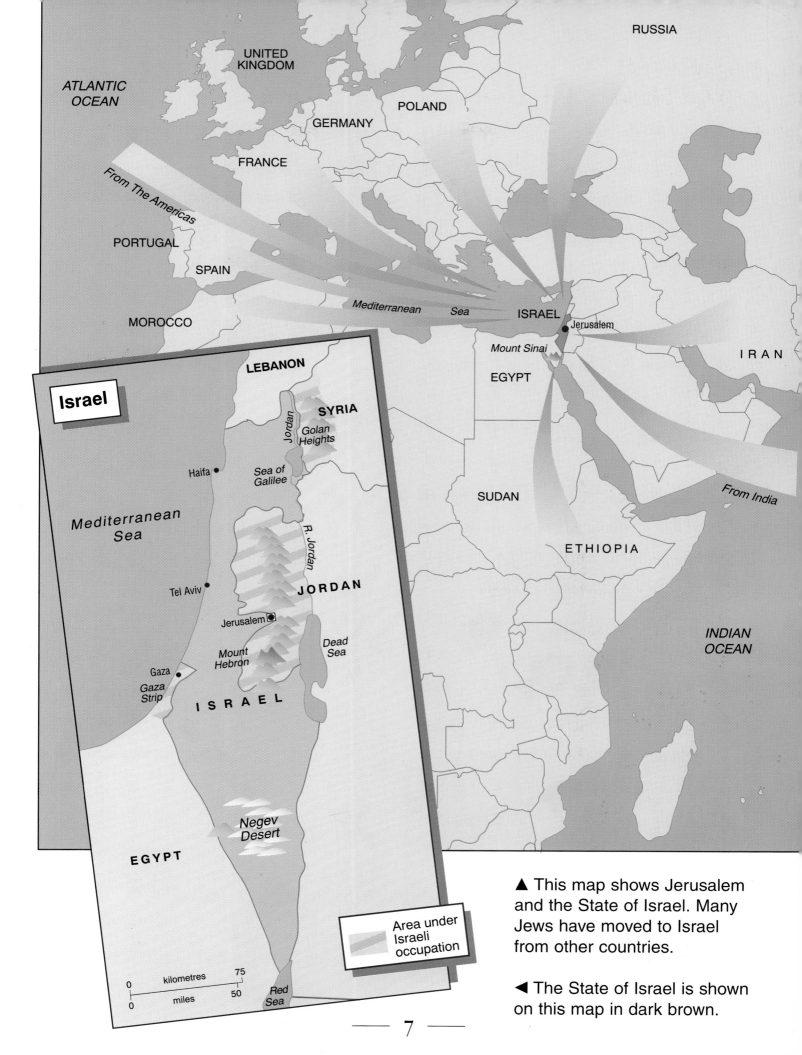

RUSSIA

ATLANTIC
OCEAN

UNITED
KINGDOM

POLAND

GERMANY

FRANCE

From The Americas

PORTUGAL

SPAIN

MOROCCO

Mediterranean   Sea

ISRAEL

Jerusalem

Mount Sinai

EGYPT

IRAN

SUDAN

From India

ETHIOPIA

INDIAN
OCEAN

Israel

LEBANON

SYRIA

Jordan

Golan
Heights

Haifa

Sea of
Galilee

Mediterranean
Sea

R. Jordan

Tel Aviv

JORDAN

Jerusalem

Dead
Sea

Mount
Hebron

Gaza

Gaza
Strip

I S R A E L

Negev
Desert

EGYPT

Area under
Israeli
occupation

0   kilometres   75

0   miles   50

Red
Sea

▲ This map shows Jerusalem
and the State of Israel. Many
Jews have moved to Israel
from other countries.

◄ The State of Israel is shown
on this map in dark brown.

— 7 —

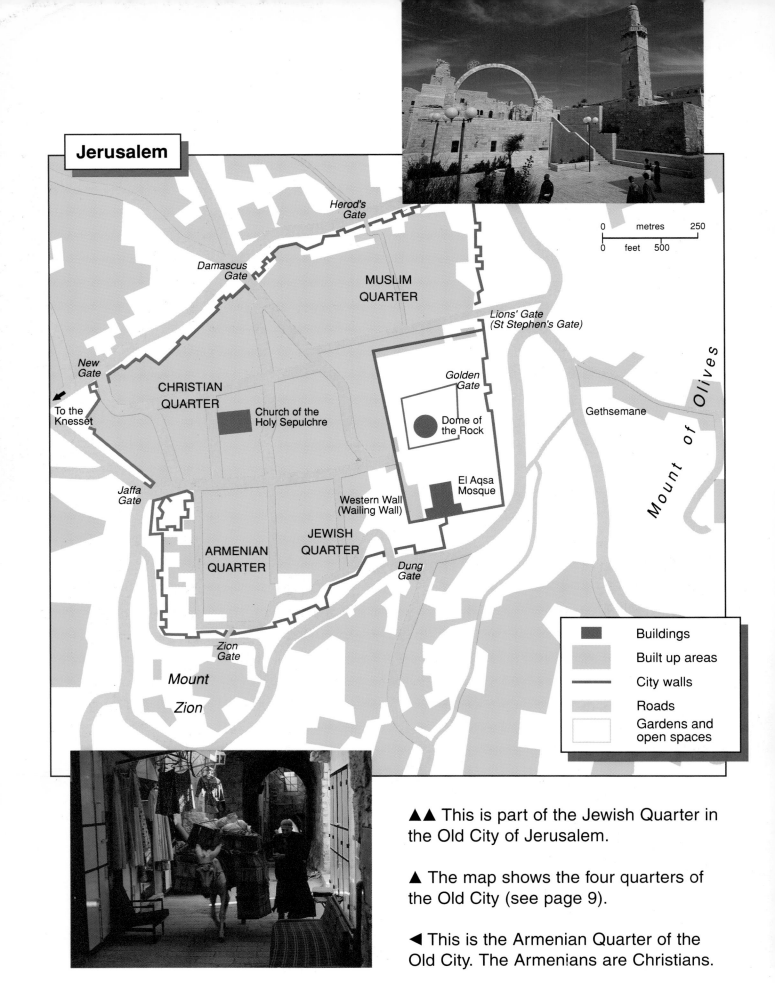

Jerusalem

Herod's Gate

Damascus Gate

MUSLIM QUARTER

Lions' Gate
(St Stephen's Gate)

New Gate

CHRISTIAN QUARTER

To the Knesset

Church of the Holy Sepulchre

Golden Gate

Dome of the Rock

Gethsemane

El Aqsa Mosque

Jaffa Gate

Western Wall
(Wailing Wall)

JEWISH QUARTER

ARMENIAN QUARTER

Dung Gate

Zion Gate

Mount

Zion

Mount of Olives

| | metres | 250 |
| 0 | feet | 500 |

Buildings

Built up areas

City walls

Roads

Gardens and open spaces

▲▲ This is part of the Jewish Quarter in the Old City of Jerusalem.

▲ The map shows the four quarters of the Old City (see page 9).

◄ This is the Armenian Quarter of the Old City. The Armenians are Christians.

A divided city

Today, Jerusalem is made up of two parts. The western part of the city is called West Jerusalem. People started building this part about 130 years ago. It became part of Israel when the State of Israel was created in 1948. Most of the people who live in West Jerusalem are Jewish. The Jewish Parliament, called the Knesset, lies in West Jerusalem.

The eastern part of Jerusalem includes the Old City. Most of the people who live in East Jerusalem are Christians or Muslim Arabs.

An old wall surrounds the Old City. Inside, there are narrow streets and small, stone houses and shops. The Old City is divided into four areas, the Armenian Quarter, the Christian Quarter, the Jewish Quarter and the Muslim Quarter (see map on page 8).

▲ This is a street market in the Muslim Quarter of the Old City of Jerusalem.

◀ These new houses are in a Jewish area of Jerusalem.

The people

Over 677,000 people live in Jerusalem. There are about 489,000 Jewish people, about 171,000 Muslim Arabs, and about 17,000 Christians. The official languages are **Hebrew** and **Arabic**. But people speak many other languages and **dialects**.

Many of the Jewish people in Jerusalem were born in the State of Israel. They are called Sabras. But many Jewish people have moved to Israel from other countries (see map on page 7). They have come from America and from eastern Europe, from North African countries such as Morocco and Ethiopia, from India and from the former Soviet Union.

▲ These priests are members of the Greek Orthodox Church. This is a Christian Church.

Key words

Arabic the language of the Arabs. There are many different dialects of Arabic.

dialects different ways of speaking the same language.

Hebrew the ancient language of the Jewish people. It is now the official language of Israel.

Think back

Look at the map of Israel on page 7. You can see that the Jews moved to Israel from many countries. Can you work out what languages they brought with them?

The birth of Jerusalem

Jerusalem lies at the edge of a desert and among rocky hills. It seems an unlikely place for people to want to live. But there is a source of fresh water at the Gihon spring, and rainfall makes the Kidron and Hinnom valleys very fertile. Early people built their homes and started to farm this **fertile** land. **Archaeologists** have found remains of these early people and their homes. From these remains, we know that people lived in this area as long as 5000 years ago.

How did this simple settlement become a holy city for the Christians, Jews and Muslims? The history of Jerusalem as a holy city starts with the life of Abraham. You can find the story of Abraham in the Torah, the holy book of the Jews and in the Christian Bible, the holy book of the Christians. It is also in the Qur'an, the holy book of the Muslims, although the story is told in a slightly different way.

Abraham

Abraham lived about 4000 years ago in a city called Ur in Mesopotamia. One day God spoke to Abraham in a dream, about a land, just like the

▼ This is one of the fertile valleys that lie to the north and west of Jerusalem. People grow almonds, olives and figs in these valleys.

valleys of Kidron and Hinnom. Abraham took his family and his flocks of sheep and started the long journey towards Canaan (now called Israel). People believe that Abraham stopped at the small settlement which later became Jerusalem.

God decided to test Abraham's faith. God told Abraham to **sacrifice** his son. Abraham took his son to the top of a hill and got ready to kill him. When God saw that Abraham was about to do it, he stopped Abraham and provided a ram to be sacrificed instead. God was satisfied that Abraham's faith was strong enough.

The 12 tribes

Abraham's son had a son called Jacob. Jacob had 12 sons who all had large families. These families, or tribes, lived from the north to the south of Canaan. They became known as the **Hebrews**.

The Hebrews suffered many hardships. They were forced to leave their homeland because of **famine**. One of their leaders was called Moses. He eventually led the Hebrews back from Egypt to their homeland. God promised the Hebrews that they could live in their 'Promised Land' if they obeyed His laws. God gave these laws to Moses. The most important were called the Ten Commandments, and they were written on two stone tablets. Moses had a box made for the tablets called the Ark of the Covenant.

◄ This scroll contains the Torah, the holy book of the Jews. The Ten Commandments and other laws are written down in the Torah.

Kings and palaces

A Hebrew king called David turned Jerusalem into an important city. He made it a home for the Ark of the Covenant. Later, his son, King Solomon, built a beautiful Temple where people could worship God and where the Ark was kept. Solomon also built many palaces and made Jerusalem into a busy city for trade.

▼ This is the fortress known as the Tower of David. It is 2000 years old and was used to defend Jerusalem until the 20th-century.

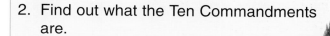

Key words

archaeologist someone who studies the past by examining objects and remains of peoples and their settlements.

exile when people are forced to live outside their home country.

famine when there is not enough food to keep people alive.

fertile describes land where plants grow well.

Hebrews another word for Jewish people.

sacrifice to kill an animal or a person to show your faith in gods or God.

Think back

1. According to the Bible, why did God stop Abraham sacrificing his son?

2. Find out what the Ten Commandments are.

Sharing Jerusalem

Jews, Christians and Muslims share the story of Abraham. But each religion also has its own link with Jerusalem.

Jerusalem and the Jews
Jerusalem is special for the Jews because it is the centre of their religion. They see it as a city built to the glory of God.

Over many centuries, the Jews scattered to many parts of the world (see page 22). But the Jewish religion did not die. **Scholars** explained the laws of the Torah in a book called the Talmud, telling Jews how they should live and worship. Jews in all parts of the world followed the laws in the Torah and the Talmud. They kept the Jewish religion and ways

▲ This is a model of Jerusalem as it may have looked at the time of King Herod.

of life alive.

For many hundreds of years, Jewish people waited for the time when they could return to Jerusalem. Today, many Jews once again live in their 'Promised Land'.

Jerusalem and the Christians
In 63 BCE, the Romans conquered **Palestine** and renamed it Judea. They made a local Jew, called Herod, King of Judea. But the Jewish people did not like Herod. They prayed that a holy person, a messiah, would come to save them.

◀ Schoolchildren helping the **rabbi** to roll up a Torah scroll.

Christians believe that Jesus Christ was the Messiah.

One day some wise men came to see Herod. They told him about the birth of a baby who would be a new king. Herod acted quickly. He sent his soldiers to kill every new-born baby in Judea. But one baby and his parents escaped to Egypt. This baby was Jesus.

When Jesus grew up he returned to Judea. He told people about God's love, and that they must try to be kind and loving. When Jesus went to Jerusalem to celebrate the Jewish Feast of Passover (see page 34), crowds cheered and clapped him. But many of the Jewish leaders were afraid of Jesus. They plotted against him. Eventually the Roman governor of Judea, Pontius Pilate, sentenced Jesus to death.

▼ The mother of a Bedouin family prepares a meal. Most of the nomads in Israel and surrounding countries are Muslims.

Jesus died on a wooden cross. Christians believe that three days later, Jesus rose from the dead. This is called the resurrection. Jesus spent his last days in Jerusalem, so it is not surprising that the city is a holy place for Christians.

Jerusalem and the Muslims

In 570 CE a man called Muhammad was born in the city of Makkah, which lies in present-day Saudi Arabia.

When he grew up, Muhammad became a **merchant**. Everywhere he

went he was known for his honesty and goodness. He was a thoughtful man, and he often went to a cave in the mountains near Makkah to sit and pray. One day, an angel appeared to him and gave him a message from God (**Allah**). This was the first of many messages. Muhammad began to tell people in Makkah about the messages from Allah. Later, followers of Muhammad wrote these messages down to form the Qur'an, the holy book of the Muslims.

◄ This is the Ka'bah shrine in Makkah.

16

◄ This beautiful Qur'an is decorated with Arabic writing. It was made nearly 1300 years ago.

Key words

Allah the Arabic word for God.

Bedouin people who move from place to place looking for food and grazing for their animals.

merchant a person who buys and sells goods.

Palestine the area between the River Jordan and the Mediterranean Sea (see map on page 7). Palestine was divided between Israel and Jordan in 1948.

prophets messengers of God.

rabbi a Jewish teacher and religious leader.

scholars people who have studied hard.

The Qur'an tells of Muhammad's Night Journey. One night, an angel woke Muhammad and gave him an animal (often described as a winged horse). As fast as lightning the animal took Muhammad to Jerusalem. In Jerusalem Muhammad met and led other **prophets** in prayer. Muhammad rose into the heavens and to the prescence of Allah. By the next morning, Muhammad was back in Makkah. Because of Muhammad's Night Journey, Jerusalem became a holy city for Muslims.

Think back

1. Why is Jerusalem a special city for Christians?

2. What is a Qur'an?

Jerusalem lost

King Solomon died in about 931 BCE. After this time some Jews began to worship other gods. Others argued with each other about how they should rule Israel. Jerusalem became weak, and many people attacked the city.

Battles for Jerusalem

In 586 BCE Nebuchadnezzar of Babylon attacked Jerusalem. His army burned the city and destroyed Solomon's Temple. After this many different kingdoms and empires ruled over Jerusalem. The Jews regained control of their city only twice. The first time they built a new, smaller Temple in

▲ A lamp is lit as part of the Hanukkah celebrations (see page 34).

516 BCE. The second time was in 164 BCE. The Jews **reconsecrated** the Temple with much joy and happiness. Jews still celebrate this event in a festival called Hanukkah (see page 34).

Romans in Jerusalem

In 70 CE the Romans attacked Jerusalem. They destroyed the Temple, as well as palaces, theatres and houses. For 60 years Jerusalem lay in ruins.

◀ This stone carving shows an Egyptian goddess Isis with her child Horus. It comes from Ashkelon, about 60 kilometres from Jerusalem.

Then a new Roman ruler, Hadrian, decided to build a new city on top of the old one. The Jews tried to rebel against the Romans between 132 CE and 135, but they were unsuccessful. After this the Romans would not allow Jews to live in Jerusalem.

Around this time Christianity was a very new religion. At first, Christians worshipped in the same buildings as Jews. But later they started to meet in their own places of worship called churches. The Romans **persecuted** Jews and Christians alike.

▲ These Roman remains are in Jerusalem. They are the ruins of the Roman city built by Hadrian.

Christians in Jerusalem

Things changed for the Christians when the Roman Emperor Constantine came to power. Constantine supported Christianity and in 313 CE he allowed Christians to worship openly. Jerusalem became part of Constantine's Christian Empire.

Constantine's mother was called Helena. She was a very religious woman. She travelled to Jerusalem to visit Jesus's tomb. In a cave near Golgotha she discovered a cross. She believed that this was the cross on which Jesus died. She built

◄ These gold coins were used in Jerusalem some time around 164 BCE.

a church on the spot and put part of the cross inside it. This church was called the Church of the Holy Sepulchre. People came from all over the world to worship in this church.

The Islamic city of Jerusalem

By the 600s CE, most of the people in the countries around Palestine were Muslims. In 638, a Muslim **Khaliph** (leader) called Omar decided to make Jerusalem a Muslim city. The Christians ruled the city, but they were tired and weak after many years of battles and wars. So they did not fight when Omar entered the city. Omar rode into Jerusalem on a camel. He did not take any soldiers with him, only a **companion** carrying a supply of dates.

Omar let both Christians and Jews live in the city. Christians and Jews were also allowed to follow their own religions. But all Christians and Jews had to pay a special tax to the Muslim rulers and were protected in return.

The Crusades

In 1096 the leaders of the Christian Church in the West decided to start a war against the Muslims. They sent Christian soldiers to attack the Muslims in Jerusalem. These wars were called the Crusades.

The soldiers of the First Crusade attacked and

◀ Some people believe that this is Jesus's tomb in the Church of the Holy Sepulchre.

◄ This map of Jerusalem is nearly 1700 years old. It is a mosaic map, made from tiny pieces of coloured glass and tile.

Key words

companion someone who keeps you company when you are on your own.

Khaliph the title of the ruler of the Islamic world after the prophet Muhammad.

massacre to kill many people in one place.

persecute to be cruel and unjust to someone.

reconsecrated if you consecrate a place you make it holy through a special ceremony. If you reconsecrate it, you make it holy again.

destroyed Jerusalem. They **massacred** thousands of Muslims and Jews. But their rule lasted only until 1187. Then the great Muslim leader, Saladin, finally threw the Christians out of Jerusalem.

► The Crusaders built these pillars. They are part of the entrance to the Church of the Holy Sepulchre.

The Diaspora

The word 'Diaspora' means 'scattering'. It describes the way that most of the Jews split into different groups and went to different parts of the world. They did this because other people attacked and invaded their homeland.

The Babylonians destroyed Jerusalem in 586 BCE. They took thousands of Jews to Babylon. The Jewish **exiles** in Babylon worked hard to keep their Jewish faith alive. They wrote down the history and traditions of the Jews. They held prayer meetings in people's homes, because there was no Temple to worship in.

A Jewish prophet called Isaiah prepared the exiles for their return to Jerusalem. In 539 BCE, the Persians conquered the Babylonians. The King of Persia, Cyrus, allowed the Jews to move back to Jerusalem. The Jews built a new Temple to replace Solomon's Temple (see page 13).

In later years, the Jews were forced into exile again. But they took with them a strong Jewish faith. Wherever they went, they worshipped according to their holy books. Each year, at the Feast of Passover, Jews all over the world celebrated the time when Moses led the Hebrews out of Egypt (see page 12). This is still an important celebration for all Jews. At the Passover meal, the head of each family says "Le shana haba'a bi Yerushalaim" which is Hebrew for "Next year in Jerusalem".

▼ A Jewish family celebrates the Feast of Passover.

Key words

exiles describes people who are in exile, forced to live away from their homeland.

A nation for the Jews

Over the centuries, small groups of Jews always managed to stay in the area of Jerusalem. However, most of the people in this region were Muslim Arabs. But by 1914, there were 85,000 Jews living in Palestine.

Jews in Palestine and all over the world were looking for a homeland for their people. They wanted a place where Jews could live and worship together without fear. Muslim people had lived in Palestine for many hundreds of years. Many Palestinian people did not want a Jewish nation in Palestine.

There was a lot of fighting and, in 1947, the **United Nations** made a plan. They wanted to divide Palestine into two countries: one Jewish and one Muslim. They also wanted to make Jerusalem an international city where people of all religions could worship safely.

The Muslims did not agree with this, and in 1948, Jews and Muslims went to war. The Jews declared part of Palestine

▲ Many buildings have been destroyed during the wars in Jerusalem.

to be the new State of Israel and won the western part of Jerusalem. The Muslims took the eastern part. In 1950, the Jews made the western part of Jerusalem, West Jerusalem, the capital of Israel. In 1967, after another war, Israel took control of the whole of the city of Jerusalem.

Key words

United Nations an international organisation that promotes peace and cooperation between all the countries of the world.

Jewish places of worship

◄ People push pieces of paper with prayers written on them into the cracks between stones in the Western Wall.

The Western Wall

Jerusalem is the most important city for Jews all over the world. One of the reasons it is so important is the Western Wall, sometimes called the Wailing Wall, on Temple Mount. Jews believe that this wall is the only part of the Temple that was left after the Romans destroyed Jerusalem in 70 CE (see page 18). Many layers of rubble and old buildings lie beneath the Wall. Deep down, Solomon's Temple is one of these buildings. Many Jews think that the Ark of the Covenant (see page 13) is buried in the ruins of this Temple. All of this makes the Western Wall a very special, sacred place.

Jews once came to Temple Mount to weep at the destruction of their Temple. They used to pray that Jerusalem would become their city again. Today, Jews control the whole of Jerusalem. They come to the Wall to pray and celebrate. Many people write prayers on pieces of paper and push the paper into cracks between the stones. Others come to read from the Torah. Everyone who comes to the Western Wall must wear the right clothes. Men wear head coverings, and women cover their shoulders.

▲ A Bar Mitzvah ceremony at the Western Wall. The boy is carrying a Torah scroll.

A place for celebration

When a Jewish girl is 12 years old, and a Jewish boy is 13, they have special celebrations. The ceremony for girls is called Bat Mitzvah or 'Daughter of the Commandment'. The ceremony for boys is called Bar Mitzvah, or 'Son of the Commandment'. These ceremonies mark the start of adult religious life for these girls and boys.

Some parents like to hold the Bar Mitzvah ceremony at the Western Wall.

▶ A Bar Mitzvah ceremony inside part of the Yohanan Ben Zakkai Synagogue.

▲ Ultra-Orthodox Jews in the streets of Me'a She'arim

Synagogues
Over many hundreds of years, Jews came back from all over the world to live in Jerusalem. These settlers soon began to build **synagogues**. Many synagogues show the styles and customs of the lands the Jews had left behind.

Old synagogues
One very old synagogue is called the Ramban Synagogue. It is named after a Jew called Ramban. He returned from Spain to live with the small group of Jews who had stayed in Palestine. The Jews were allowed to build this synagogue in the 1200s CE. It still stands in the Jewish Quarter of the Old City.

The Jerusalem Great Synagogue
The Jerusalem Great Synagogue was opened in 1983. It is in West Jerusalem. Jews go there to worship on Shabbat (the Sabbath), which is on Saturday. Jews believe that God told Moses to keep this day of the week holy.

Close to this synagogue is the area called Me'a She'arim, which means 'One Hundred Gates'. This is one of the homes of **ultra-Orthodox** Jews. These Jews live according to strict, religious rules. People who visit this area must follow the customs of the local people. For example, women must wear long skirts and long sleeves.

Yad Vashem
In West Jerusalem there is a special building in memory of the six million Jews killed in the **Holocaust** during World War II. The German Nazis rounded up the Jewish

▲ These young boys are reading prayers at school. Notice the Torah scrolls in the background.

► Inside Yad Vashem there are displays to show the suffering of the Jewish prisoners in the death camps.

people in Germany and other countries that they occupied in Europe. They sent millions of Jews to death camps and murdered them. The memorial building is called Yad Vashem and it sits on Memorial Hill. Inside, there are displays to explain what happened to the Jewish people during the Holocaust.

Key words

Holocaust the word used to describe the murder of six million Jews by the Nazis in World War II.

synagogue a Jewish place of meeting, study and worship.

ultra-Orthodox people who live according to very strict religious rules.

Christian shrines and churches

The Church of the Holy Sepulchre

The Church of the Holy Sepulchre (see page 20) is the most important Christian **shrine** in Jerusalem. There are various chapels inside this church. They stand on the places where Christians believe that Jesus was crucified, buried and resurrected (see page 16). **Pilgrims** have come to this sacred place since the beginning of Christianity.

Helena, the mother of Emperor Constantine (see page 19), started building the Church of the Holy Sepulchre in 326 CE. For years this church was the most splendid in the whole world. But in 614 the Persians destroyed it. The Crusaders rebuilt much of the church in 1149. Since then,

▲ Monks pray in the chapel built over the place where Jesus died on the cross.

there have been earthquakes and fires, and parts of the church have been repaired. Today, many different Christian groups look after the Church of the Holy Sepulchre.

Easter rituals during Holy week

Christians believe that the day before he died, Jesus and his

◄ These domes and towers are all part of the Church of the Holy Sepulchre.

disciples sat down to a meal. This is called the Last Supper. It is remembered by Christians on the Thursday of **Holy Week**, called Maundy Thursday. Maundy means 'command' or 'ask'. At the Last Supper, Jesus asked his disciples to remember him in the breaking of bread and drinking wine.

Before the Last Supper, Jesus washed the feet of his disciples. He told the disciples that they, too, must wash the feet of others in the same way. Every year, on Maundy Thursday, Christian priests follow Jesus's example. In the Catholic Church in Jerusalem, the High Priest bathes the feet of his priests.

Good Friday is the day when Christians remember Jesus's death on the cross (see page 16). Christians believe that He walked from Herod's palace in Jerusalem to Golgotha where the cross stood. This walk is called the Via Dolorosa, the walk of sorrow. It ends at Jesus's tomb in the Church of the Holy Sepulchre. There are 14 stops on the Via Dolorosa. Christians call these stops the 'stations of the cross'. They are places where people believe Jesus stopped, or where things happened to him. Pilgrims stop at these holy stations to pray.

▲ On Good Friday, crowds of people walk along the Via Dolorosa. Some people carry a cross, just as Jesus did.

The last station is Jesus's tomb.

Not all Christian pilgrims can come to Jerusalem at Easter. So there is a pilgrimage walk along the Via Dolorosa every Friday of the year.

Other churches

One of the most loved Christian shrines is the Basilica of The Agony. This church was built in 1924. It stands in the Garden of Gethsemane. Christians believe that Jesus prayed in this garden on the night before his death. Some people call this church the Church of All Nations. This is because Christians from all over the world sent money to help build it.

A short distance from Gethsemane, pilgrims can visit Mary's tomb. Mary was the mother of Jesus. Pilgrims have come to her tomb for centuries. The walls are black with smoke from their candles.

▲ This is the Russian Church of Mary Magdalene in Jerusalem. It was built in 1888. Mary Magdelene was a friend and a follower of Jesus.

▲ The Church of All Nations stands in the Garden of Gethsemane. The name Gethsemane means 'olive press'. Old olive trees still grow in this garden.

Key words

disciple a follower. Jesus chose 12 disciples to learn from him and to spread his teachings.

Holy Week the week in the Christian calendar that starts with Palm Sunday and ends with Easter Sunday.

pilgrim someone who travels to a holy place for religious reasons.

shrine a holy place where people go to pray and worship.

Think back

1. Why do you think Jesus bathed the feet of his disciples? What do you think he was trying to teach them?

2. What do pilgrims do on the Via Dolorosa?

3. What did Jesus ask his followers to do to remember him?

Mosques of Jerusalem

Muslims think of Jerusalem as one of the three holiest cities with Makkah and Madinah. There are many mosques in Jerusalem. They are used for prayer and learning, as they are all over the world. Each mosque has a leader, or imam, who leads the prayers.

Muslims worship five times a day. A person known as a muezzin calls Muslims to prayer from a tall tower, or

▼ The tall tower on this mosque is called a minaret. A muezzin calls Muslims to prayer from the minaret.

▲ The Dome of the Rock has a shiny golden roof. This is made from pure gold (see page 33).

minaret. Before going into a mosque, all Muslims must wash and also take off their shoes. Muslims stand, kneel and bow down in a certain order as they say their prayers. All Muslims face in the direction of the holy city, Makkah, at prayer time. In every mosque there is a small alcove to show the right direction. This alcove is called the mihrab.

The Dome and al Aqsa Mosque

The Dome of the Rock covers the spot where the Prophet Muhammad is believed to have risen to heaven (see page 17). Nearby there is another building called the Dome of the Chain.

The central mosque of Jerusalem is called al Aqsa Mosque. Pilgrims to the Dome come to al Aqsa Mosque to say their prayers. The most holy day of the week for Muslims is Friday. Every Friday you can see Muslims going to al Aqsa for their special midday

▼ The main mosque in Jerusalem is al Aqsa Mosque.

▲ This is the Tomb of Joseph and the Mosque of Abraham.

worship.

There are a lot of other mosques in Jerusalem. However, Muslims do not have to go to the mosque to pray. They pray at home, at work or in the street if there is no mosque nearby.

Think back
1. Which are the special holy days of the week for Jews, Christian and Muslims? What happens on these special days?
2. Design a Muslim prayer mat. Muslims do not draw pictures of human beings or animals, so your design should include only patterns, buildings or plants.

Celebrations

Jewish festivals

The Jewish New Year is in September or October. It is called Rosh Hashanah. Jews have a two-day holiday. This holiday is the beginning of ten days **penance**. This is a time for people to show that they are sorry for their sins. At the end of the ten days there is a solemn **fast** day. This is called Yom Kippur, the Day of Atonement. On this day Jews go to the synagogue. They pray for forgiveness for their sins.

Sukkot is another festival that takes place in September or October. Sukkot is also called the Feast of Tabernacles. During Sukkot people remember the life of the Hebrews in the desert, after they had escaped from Egypt (see page 12).

Hanukkah is in November or December. This festival celebrates the reconsecration of the Temple in 164 BCE (see page 18). A huge candlestick with nine branches is lit by the Western Wall. This candlestick is called a hanukiah. People light a smaller hanukiah in their homes, too.

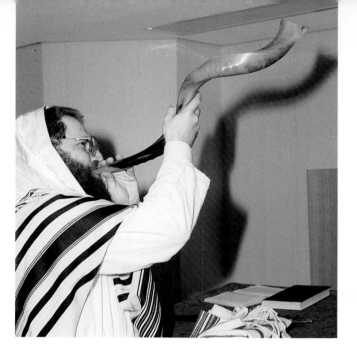

▲▲ A Jewish man blows a ram's horn during the festival of Rosh Hashanah. The ram's horn is called a shofar.

▲ People celebrating the festival of Sukkot.

At Pesach, or Passover, Jews give thanks to God. Pesach is in March or April. Jews remember the last night in Egypt before the Hebrews escaped (see page 12).

Christian festivals

Easter Sunday is the most important Christian Festival.

On this day, Christians celebrate Jesus rising from the dead (see page 16). Christmas is another important date in the Christian calendar. On this day, many pilgrims go to Bethlehem, just outside Jerusalem. This is where people believe Jesus was born.

Muslim festivals

The ninth month of the Muslim year is called Ramadan. At this time, Muslims remember the time when Muhammad first began to receive messages from Allah (see page 16). During Ramadan, Muslims do not eat or drink from before dawn until dusk. At the end of Ramadan there is a feast called

▲ These Muslim children are dressed in their best clothes for the feast of Id ul-Fitr.

Id ul-Fitr. Muslims celebrate the end of fasting by cooking and eating rich food. People put on new clothes and go to the mosque to say special prayers. Children get money and presents from their parents.

▼ Christians believe that this is the place where Christ was born, in Bethlehem. The silver star (right) marks the exact spot.

Key words

fast a fast is when you don't eat or drink. People usually fast for religious reasons.

penance a way of showing that you are sorry for something you have done.

Legends and traditions

The centre of the world

In 691 CE, Khaliph Adb el-Malik built a huge dome over the sacred rock where Muhammad is believed to have sat on his Night Journey (see page 17). He covered this dome in gold. This building is called the Dome of the Rock. Many Jews believe that the holy rock inside the Dome of the Rock is the centre of the world. They think that the Ark of the Covenant (see page 12) lies buried beneath the rock.

The walls of Jerusalem

The Old City of Jerusalem is surrounded by huge walls. The walls were built between 1537 and 1540. The great Muslim ruler Suleiman the Magnificent gave orders for the walls to be rebuilt. People say that Suleiman dreamed he would be eaten by lions if he did not rebuild the walls.

Tombs of Jerusalem

The Kidron Valley lies between Temple Mount and the Mount of Olives. This area is full of **tombs**, some old and some new. This is because many Jews have wanted to be buried in Jerusalem.

People once thought that two of the ancient tombs were those of Zechariah and Absalom. These tombs became shrines because Zechariah and Absalom are both in the Bible. But we now know that these

▼ This is the huge rock inside the Dome of the Rock, on Mount Moriah.

▲ There are eight gates in the walls of Jerusalem. This is the Lions' Gate. You can see lions carved on either side of the gate.

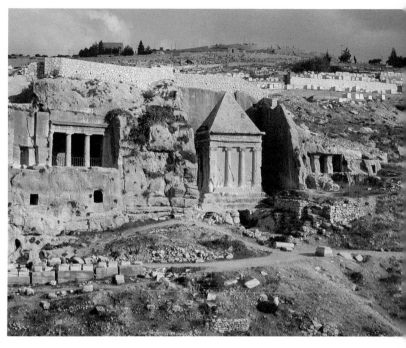

tombs are those of other Jews.

The tomb of Jesus
No-one knows exactly where Jesus was buried. Today people visit the Church of the Holy Sepulchre (see page 20) and the Garden Tomb.

▲ People once thought that these tombs were those of Zechariah and Absalom.

Key words

tomb a place where a person is buried.

Think back

1. Why is the Dome of the Rock special for Jews and Muslims?

2. Who ordered the walls of Jerusalem to be rebuilt?

Art and architecture

Over the centuries, Muslims, Jews and Christians have all brought different styles of art and **architecture** to Jerusalem. Some of the finest old works are in mosques, synagogues and churches. There are also good examples of modern art and architecture.

Four synagogues together

There are four synagogues on Mishmeret Ha-Kehuna Street. They are all connected together. The two oldest synagogues were built nearly 400 years ago. They are the Elijah the Prophet and the

▼ Inside the Yohanan Ben Zakkai Synagogue. This is one of the four, connected synagogues on Mishmeret Ha-Kehuna Street.

Yohanan Ben Zakkai synagogues. These buildings are low because the ruling Muslims did not allow Jewish or Christian buildings to be taller than Muslim ones. In the Elijah the Prophet Synagogue there is a beautiful carved wooden ark. It came from an Italian synagogue which was destroyed in World War II.

A Christian cathedral

The Cathedral of St James lies in the Armenian Quarter (see map page 8). There is a wooden board near the front door of the cathedral. When the Muslim Turks ruled Jerusalem, they did not allow Christians to ring church bells. So the Christians beat on the board to tell people when to

go to church. Outside the cathedral there is a courtyard with a beautiful fountain.

▲ These beautiful tiles cover the outside walls of the Dome of the Rock.

Islamic art

Muslims do not draw pictures of animals or humans. So they make very beautiful designs with **geometrical** patterns, flowers or Arabic script (writing). The Dome of the Rock and the al Aqsa Mosque are good examples of Muslim art and architecture.

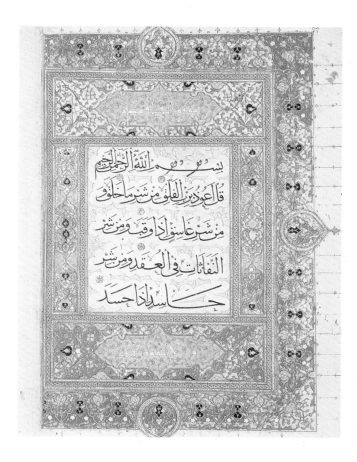

► This is a beautifully decorated page from the Qur'an. You can see the Arabic script (writing) in the centre.

Between the Dome of the Rock and al Aqsa Mosque there is a water fountain. The fountain is called al Kas, or 'The Cup'. This is where Muslims wash themselves before they go to the mosque. Nearby is the Islamic Museum. The Museum displays Islamic art, beautiful copies of the Qur'an, and colourful tiles.

Ancient art in Jerusalem

The Romans destroyed most of Jerusalem in 70 CE. But in 1979, an archaeologist found the ruins of a group of houses. These houses are 2000 years old. One of the houses obviously belonged to someone very rich. There were mosaics, wall paintings, courtyards, fine glassware and many other beautiful objects. The owner of the house was also very religious. We know this because there were private mikvehs, or baths for special religious washing. Archaeologists think that the house belonged to a wealthy high priest.

New art in Jerusalem

The Knesset is the parliament building of the State of Israel. It is in West Jerusalem. It is a good example of modern architecture in Jerusalem. In the main hall there are three tapestries by the famous artist Marc Chagall. The **tapestries** show the creation of humans, the escape of the Hebrews from Egypt, and Jerusalem itself. Outside the building is a flame which burns all the time. This flame **commemorates** the soldiers who have died in Israel's wars. Opposite the main gate there is a huge menorah. This seven-branched candleholder is the national symbol of the State of Israel.

◄ These are the ruins of houses built about 2000 years ago in Jerusalem.

▲ The Dead Sea Scrolls are kept in a building called the Shrine of the Book. One of the Scrolls lies inside this container.

Israel Museum

The Israel Museum contains works of art by Jews, and by people of other religions. One of the most important places in the museum is the Shrine of the Book. Inside the Shrine of the Book are the Dead Sea Scrolls. These are ancient writings that include parts of the Bible. They were found in 1947 in a desert cave. People think they are more than 2000 years old.

▲ This wall just outside Jerusalem is covered with bright paintings. Beyond it you can see the modern flats of West Jerusalem.

Key words

architecture the art of designing buildings, or the style in which a building is designed and decorated.

commemorate to remember something in a special way.

geometrical shapes with angles, such as squares and triangles.

tapestries pictures made out of thousands of sewn stitches.

Food in Jerusalem

You can find a wide variety of food in Jerusalem. Over the centuries, many people have moved to Jerusalem from other countries. They have brought with them new foods and new ways of cooking.

Kosher

Many Jews eat only 'kosher' food. When food is kosher, it is prepared and eaten according to the laws written in the Torah. The laws say that Jews must not eat pork, shellfish or **game**. They must not eat meat and dairy products, such as milk and cheese, together.

▲ This well-stocked fruit stall is in West Jerusalem.

▼ This is a snack bar in Jerusalem. It sells falafels which are spicy chickpea balls served in pitta bread, and lots of salad.

Halal

Muslims eat only 'halal' meat. This meat is prepared according to instructions given in the Qur'an. The Qur'an also says that Muslims must not eat pork or drink alcohol.

Breakfast

In Jerusalem breakfast is usually a big meal. People eat fresh fruit, eggs, pickled vegetables, olives, tomatoes, yoghurt and cheese. They drink fruit juice and coffee. Some people also eat hummus. This is a delicious paste made from crushed chickpeas, oil and garlic.

Lunch

For many people in Jerusalem, lunch is the main meal of the day. Muslim Arabs prefer lamb dishes. The most popular lamb dish is probably shwarma. This is a lamb kebab – pieces of lamb cooked on a metal spike. People eat it with a spicy salad.

Dinner

Most people in Jerusalem have a small meal in the evening. It is usually a simple salad or sandwiches. But sometimes

▲ Hummus is a popular dish in Jerusalem. You can eat it with pitta bread.

people go to a restaurant to eat. Then they have a large meal with a sweet desert. The most popular cake is baclava. This is flaky pastry filled with ground nuts and honey.

Key words

game animals or birds that are hunted for their meat.

Think back

Imagine you are planning a meal for three friends. One is a Jew, one is a Christian and one is a Muslim. What foods must you avoid? What will you give them for main course, pudding, and to drink?

Important events in the history of Jerusalem

BCE Before the Common Era

3000   First settlements on the site of Jerusalem

2150-1550   Time of Abraham, Isaac and Jacob

1550-1250   Hebrews go to Egypt. Moses leads them out of Egypt. He receives the commandments, later written down in the Torah. The Hebrews spend the next 40 years travelling to their 'Promised Land'.

1025   Saul becomes first King of Israel

1000   David becomes King of Israel. He conquers Jebusa, known afterwards as Jerusalem. He brings the Ark of the Covenant to the city.

968   Solomon become King of Israel. He builds the first Temple.

931   Death of Solomon.

722   Assyrians destroy Kingdom of Israel. Jews sent into exile.

586   Babylonians capture Jerusalem. Temple is destroyed. Jews are exiled to Babylon where Jewish laws are written down.

539   Persians take over Jerusalem. Jews are allowed back to Jerusalem.

516   Jews build the Second Temple.

332   Persian Empire defeated by Alexander the Great, ruler of Greek Empire.

164   Reconsecration of Temple.

63   Romans take over and rule for next 400 years.

37   Herod the Great becomes King of Judea.

5-6   Birth of Jesus Christ

CE In the Common Era

29   Jesus celebrates Passover in Jerusalem. He is arrested and put to death on a cross.

66	Jewish War against the Romans.
70	Romans destroy the Second Temple.
132	Jews rebel against Romans.
135	Emperor Hadrian rebuilds Jerusalem.
313	Emperor Constantine makes Jerusalem part of Christian Empire.
326	Helena, mother of Emperor Constantine, starts building of Church of the Holy Sepulchre.
c.570	Birth of Muhammad.
614	Persian invasion of Jerusalem. Many churches destroyed.
622	Muhammad goes from Makkah to Madinah. Islamic religion is established and Muslim Empire starts to grow.
632	Death of Prophet Muhammad. Muslim Arab empire now ruled by leader called a Khaliph.
638	Jerusalem taken over by Muslim Khaliph Omar.
691	Khaliph Abd el-Malik builds Dome of the Rock.
775-1071	Jerusalem ruled by three different Muslim empires.
1096	First Christian Crusade. Christians conquer Jerusalem and massacre Jews and Muslims.
1187	Muslim leader Saladin defeats Second Crusade and retakes Jerusalem.
1492	Jews driven out of Spain. Later, many return to Jerusalem.
1537-40	Suleiman rebuilds walls of Jerusalem.
1700	Eastern European Jews arrive in Jerusalem.
1831	Ibrahim Pasha, Muslim from Egypt, takes control of Palestine.
1840	Egyptians pushed out of Jerusalem by Turkey with backing of France and Great Britain.
1882	Arrival of first modern Jewish settlers.
1917	Defeat of Turks in World War I. British take over Jerusalem.
1948	Jews declare the State of Israel.
1967	Israel takes control of all of Jerusalem.
1973	Israel fights off Egyptian and Syrian armies.

Index

Abraham 11, 12
Arabic 10
Ark of the Covenant 12, 13, 24, 36
Armenian Quarter 8, 9

Bar Mitzvah 25
Bat Mitzvah 25
Bedouins 15
Bible 11

Christian Quarter 9
Christmas 35
Church of All Nations 30
Church of the Holy Sepulchre 20, 21, 28, 29
Constantine, Emperor 19
Crusades, the 20

David, King 13
Dead Sea Scrolls 41
Diaspora 22
Dome of the Rock 33, 36

East Jerusalem 9, 23
Easter 28, 34-35

Garden of Gethsemane 30, 31
Good Friday 29, 30
Greek Orthodox church 10

halal 43
Hanukkah 18, 34
Hebrew language 10
Hebrews 12

Herod, King 14, 15
Holocaust 26, 27
Holy Week 29

Id ul-Fitr 35
Isaiah 22
Islamic art 39, 40
Israel Museum 41

Jacob 12
Jerusalem Great Synagogue, the 26
Jesus Christ 15, 16
Jewish Quarter 8, 9
Judean Desert 6

Ka'bah 16
Knesset 9, 40
kosher food 42

Last Supper 29

Makkah 16
Maundy Thursday 29
Moses 12, 22, 26
mosques 33
Muhammad, the Holy Prophet 16
Muhammad's Night Journey 17
Muslim Quarter 9

Nebuchadnezzar, King 18

Old City 9
Omar, Khaliph 20

Palestine 23

Passover, Feast of 15, 22, 34
prayer 32, 33
'Promised Land' 14

Qur'an 11, 16, 17

Ramadan 35
Resurrection, the 16
Romans 14, 18, 19, 24
Rosh Hashanah 34

Saladin 21
Shabbat 26
Shrine of the Book 41
Solomon, King 13, 18
State of Israel 7, 9, 10, 23
Sukkot 34
Synagogues 26, 36

Talmud 14
tapestries 40
Temple, the 13, 18, 22, 24
Temple Mount 24
Ten Commandments 12
Torah 11, 12, 14, 24, 42

ultra-Orthodox Jews 26

Via Dolorosa 29, 30

West Jerusalem 9, 23
Western Wall 24, 25

Yad Vashem 26, 27
Yom Kippur 34